Contents

River kingdom   4

Pharaohs and priests   6

Dress like an Egyptian   8

On the banks of the Nile   10

Make a shaduf   12

Living in a town   14

Make Egyptian jewellery   16

Friends and family   18

Play 'Snake'   20

Writing, counting and discovering   22

Make a lucky pendant   24

Everlasting life   26

Make a mummy mask   28

Timeline   30

Glossary   31

Index and Webfinder   32

River kingdom

The Ancient Egyptians lived in North Africa, beside the River Nile. They settled there around 10,000 years ago, when climate change turned the rest of Egypt into a hot, dry desert.

The early Egyptians

The first settlers survived by hunting and fishing. Around 5500 BC, they began to grow crops and raise animals. They built villages, and traded goods they had made. Around 3100 BC, the settlers joined together to create a rich, powerful kingdom.

Egypt stayed proud and strong for thousands of years, until Roman armies invaded in 30 BC. But there are many remains of its splendid past that still survive today, for us to admire.

▲ Many fine portraits, such as this gold mummy mask, show us what the Ancient Egyptian people looked like.

Ancient Egypt was a very large ▶ country. It took weeks to travel from one end to the other. Most of the land was empty desert. All towns and villages were close to the River Nile.

The pyramids (royal tombs) at ▶ Giza are almost 5,000 years old. The biggest of the three, known as the Great Pyramid, is nearly 146m high and is built from nearly two-and-a-half million blocks of limestone.

Mediterranean Sea

LOWER EGYPT

Alexandria

Nile Delta

SINAI

Giza
Saqqara
Memphis

Great pyramids

Step pyramid

WESTERN DESERT

EASTERN DESERT

Thebes

Hatshepsut's
temple

Abydos

Luxor

Tutankhamun's
gold death mask

Valley of
the Kings

UPPER EGYPT

Temple of Isis

Aswan
Philae

Pharaoh Rameses II's temple

Red Sea

River Nile

NUBIA

Abu Simbel

N
W — E
S

0   50   100   150km

Key
☐ Desert
▨ Irrigated land

How do we know?

Egypt's dry desert soil has preserved millions
of objects, from kings' treasures and children's
toys to books of magic spells.

Magnificent monuments
We can still see Ancient Egyptian temples and
tombs, and marvel at the skills of the workers
who made them. Statues, carvings and
wall-paintings provide pictures of Egyptian life.

Mysterious mummies
X-rays and CAT scans can 'see' inside mummies.
They show us what Ancient Egyptians looked
like, what diseases they suffered from, what
they ate and how they died.

Written records
The Egyptians' own writings let us discover their
private thoughts, hopes and fears. Past travellers
to Egypt, from 500 BC to the 20th century,
have also left detailed descriptions.

Pharaohs and priests

Powerful kings, called pharaohs, ruled Ancient Egypt. Egyptians believed that pharaohs were the sons of gods, who went to live among the stars when they died.

The power of the pharaohs

The pharaoh was the most important person in Ancient Egypt. He was the law-maker, army commander and chief priest. Pharaohs also controlled trade, taxes, mining, irrigation and food supplies. They made war, or peace, with foreign rulers, and paid for massive temples and tombs so that everyone would remember them.

Golden shrine – holy house for the god

Priest holds sweet-smelling incense

Pillars hold up the temple roof. They are decorated with carvings showing gods, pharaohs and hieroglyphics (picture-writing)

Statue of Horus, hawk-headed sky-god who protected pharaohs

Offerings to please the gods, and to ask for help and protection in return

Pharaoh prays to the god Horus

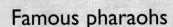

Famous pharaohs

Narmer (c. 3100 BC) First pharaoh of the united kingdom of Egypt.

Khufu (2589–2566 BC) Pharaoh who built the Great Pyramid.

Amenhotep I (1525–1504 BC) Pharaoh who conquered Nubia.

Hatshepsut (1498–1483 BC) Queen who sent traders and explorers to East Africa.

Thutmose III (1479–1425 BC) Famous warrior pharaoh who defeated the Syrians at the battle of Megiddo (Armageddon).

Akenhaten (1379–1334 BC) Pharaoh who tried to change Egyptian religion. He built a new capital city and wrote hymns.

Tutankhamun (1334–1325 BC) Died aged 18. Famous for his treasure-filled tomb in the Valley of the Kings.

Rameses II (1279–1213 BC) Defeated invaders from Turkey. Died aged 92!

Cleopatra VII (51–30 BC) Clever, charming queen who tried to stop the Roman invaders. Killed herself when she failed.

▼ Pharaohs were the living link between the Egyptian people and the gods. Pharaohs prayed to the gods and gave them offerings of food. In return, they hoped the gods would protect them.

Sistrum (little rattle, with bells)

Cymbals

Priestesses chant and play music

What they wore

This wall-painting (below) shows the pharaoh Amenemhet (with beard) with his family. Most Egyptians wore white linen clothes but the pharaoh's clothes would have been made from a finer linen. Some priests wore lion or leopard skins, magic signs of life and death, past and future.

▲ The pharaoh (with beard) and his son are wearing short, pleated kilts. The women are wearing long, straight dresses with shoulder-straps.

Dress like an Egyptian

All Ancient Egyptians, both rich and poor, wore clothes made of linen to keep cool in Egypt's hot climate. Men wore a knee-length 'kilt', knotted at the waist. Women wore long dresses, often with pleats. People mostly went barefoot, or wore sandals woven from reeds.

Tie a strip of white or gold fabric, or a ribbon, around your wig to make a headband

Vulture collar, made in the same way as the collar on page 16

Plait cords or ribbons of gold, turquoise and blue to make a belt

Turn to page 16 to find out how to make the bracelets

Make a kilt from a rectangular strip of fabric, knotted at the waist

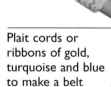

Tunic

1

Lay the fabric flat and smooth out any wrinkles. Cut out a piece measuring 60cm wide and about 200–220cm long.

Wig

1

Loop about 200, 60cm lengths of black wool on a table top, to keep them flat. If possible, keep the strands of wool the same length.

◀ Ancient Egyptians paid great attention to their appearance. Both men and women wore jewellery and used make-up, especially dramatic green or black eye paint. Rich men and women wore wigs, which were held in place with beeswax.

2

Fold the cloth in half lengthways. Measure and mark 15cm in from each edge of the fold, then cut a curved slit between the marks to make a neck hole.

3

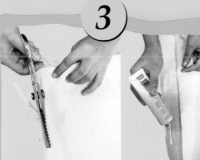

Trim the outer edges of the fabric with pinking shears to stop it fraying. Glue the long edges of the cloth together with fabric glue, leaving 25–30cm open at the top edges for armholes.

Tie the tunic at the waist with a belt of plaited cord, or ribbon.

You will need

For the tunic:
- A large piece of white fabric
- Tape measure • Scissors
- Pinking shears • Fabric glue
- Cord or ribbon

For the wig:
- A ball of thick black wool
- Scissors
- Strip of white or gold fabric, or ribbon

2

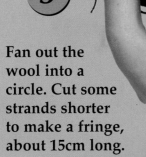

Tie a piece of wool round the centre of the looped strands and knot tightly. Cut the looped ends with scissors.

3

Fan out the wool into a circle. Cut some strands shorter to make a fringe, about 15cm long.

On the banks of the Nile

In Egypt, it hardly ever rains. So how did people survive? By making good use of the River Nile.

The river of life

The land beside the Nile was rich and fertile; farmers grew wheat and barley to make bread, and many fruits and vegetables. They raised cattle, sheep, goats, pigs, geese and ducks, for meat, milk and eggs.

Egyptians also dug mud to shape into bricks, and cut reeds to make paper, mats, baskets, sandals and boats. They washed and went swimming in the Nile, and enjoyed picnics beside it. Sailing down the river was the easiest way to travel, as there were no proper roads.

Donkeys carry loads

Houses built from bricks made from Nile mud

Goatherd and goats

Most Ancient Egyptians were farmers who lived along the banks of the River Nile.

▲ This wall-painting from an Egyptian tomb shows a family hunting wild birds among tall papyrus reeds beside the River Nile. Their pet cat is enjoying the hunt, as well!

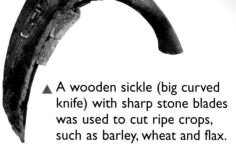
▲ A wooden sickle (big curved knife) with sharp stone blades was used to cut ripe crops, such as barley, wheat and flax.

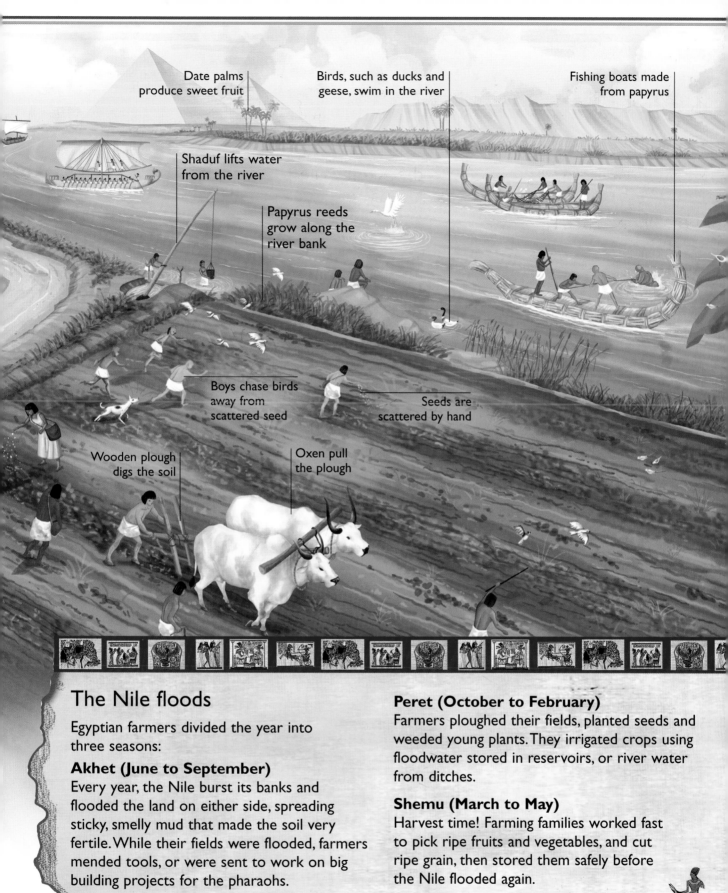

Date palms
produce sweet fruit

Birds, such as ducks and
geese, swim in the river

Fishing boats made
from papyrus

Shaduf lifts water
from the river

Papyrus reeds
grow along the
river bank

Boys chase birds
away from
scattered seed

Seeds are
scattered by hand

Wooden plough
digs the soil

Oxen pull
the plough

The Nile floods

Egyptian farmers divided the year into
three seasons:

Akhet (June to September)

Every year, the Nile burst its banks and
flooded the land on either side, spreading
sticky, smelly mud that made the soil very
fertile. While their fields were flooded, farmers
mended tools, or were sent to work on big
building projects for the pharaohs.

Peret (October to February)

Farmers ploughed their fields, planted seeds and
weeded young plants. They irrigated crops using
floodwater stored in reservoirs, or river water
from ditches.

Shemu (March to May)

Harvest time! Farming families worked fast
to pick ripe fruits and vegetables, and cut
ripe grain, then stored them safely before
the Nile flooded again.

Make a shaduf

Once the waters of the Nile went down each year, the rich, black mud started to dry out in the sun. The farmers tried to trap as much of the floodwater as possible in mud-brick reservoirs and irrigation canals. They then lifted the water from the canals to the fields using a device called a shaduf. Each shaduf could be operated by just one person. This project shows you how to make a model shaduf.

1 Find two strong, forked twigs, each around 10cm long. Press them into a ball of clay around 5–10cm apart. Leave the clay to harden overnight.

How a shaduf worked

A shaduf was a long pole balanced on a cross beam with a bucket and rope at one end and a heavy counterweight at the other. The farmer would pull the rope to lower the bucket into the canal, then raise the bucket by pushing on the weight. The pole could be swung around, so that the bucket of water could be emptied over the fields.

◄ Some Egyptian farmers still use a shaduf to water their fields.

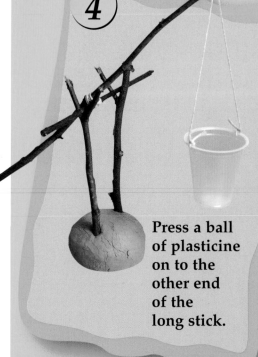

4 Press a ball of plasticine on to the other end of the long stick.

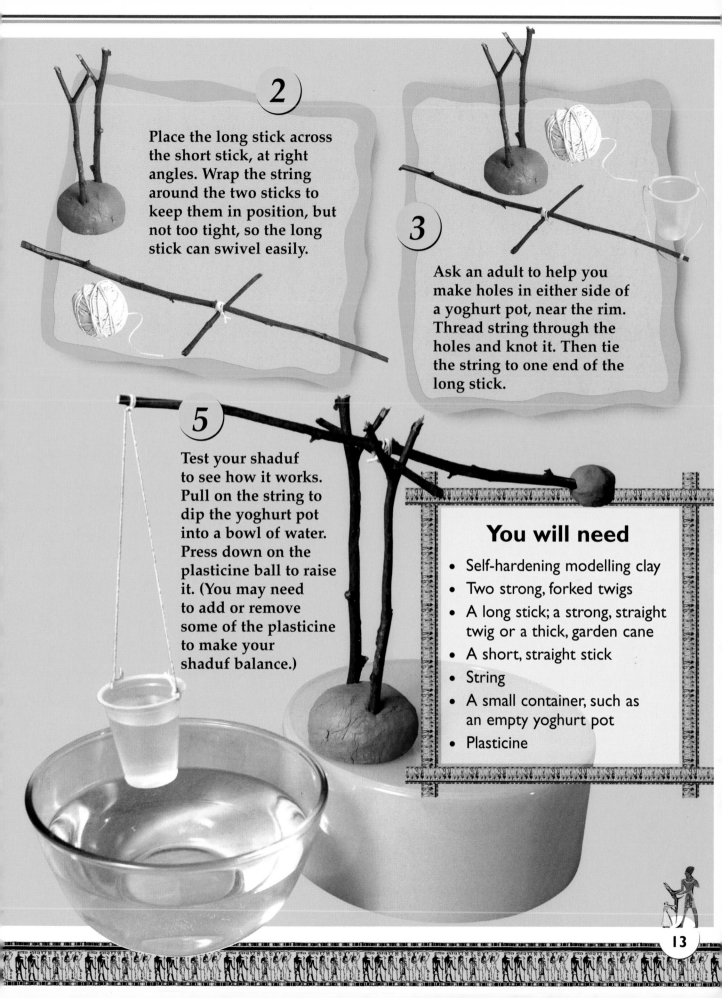

2

Place the long stick across the short stick, at right angles. Wrap the string around the two sticks to keep them in position, but not too tight, so the long stick can swivel easily.

3

Ask an adult to help you make holes in either side of a yoghurt pot, near the rim. Thread string through the holes and knot it. Then tie the string to one end of the long stick.

5

Test your shaduf to see how it works. Pull on the string to dip the yoghurt pot into a bowl of water. Press down on the plasticine ball to raise it. (You may need to add or remove some of the plasticine to make your shaduf balance.)

You will need

- Self-hardening modelling clay
- Two strong, forked twigs
- A long stick; a strong, straight twig or a thick, garden cane
- A short, straight stick
- String
- A small container, such as an empty yoghurt pot
- Plasticine

Living in a town

Most Egyptians lived in small country villages. But Egypt also had many big, busy towns, with crowded streets guarded by wooden gates and mud-brick walls.

Fishing boat

Small window-openings are secure, but make houses dark inside

Flat roofs of houses used as extra living rooms

▲ Egyptian craft-workers had workshops in towns. It took many years to learn how to carve stone into statues, or how to make jewellery, pottery, glass and metal containers or fine linen cloth.

All towns had markets selling food and ▲ drink, and useful goods that ordinary Egyptians could not make themselves, such as sandals or pottery.

Busy centres

Some towns were holy places, where people came to pray to their favourite gods. Others were government centres; the pharaoh's officials and tax collectors lived there. A few towns were purpose-built to house workers making and decorating royal tombs.

Craftsmen and women worked in ▶ the open air, or in crowded workshops behind houses in towns. This model shows carpenters hard at work in their shop.

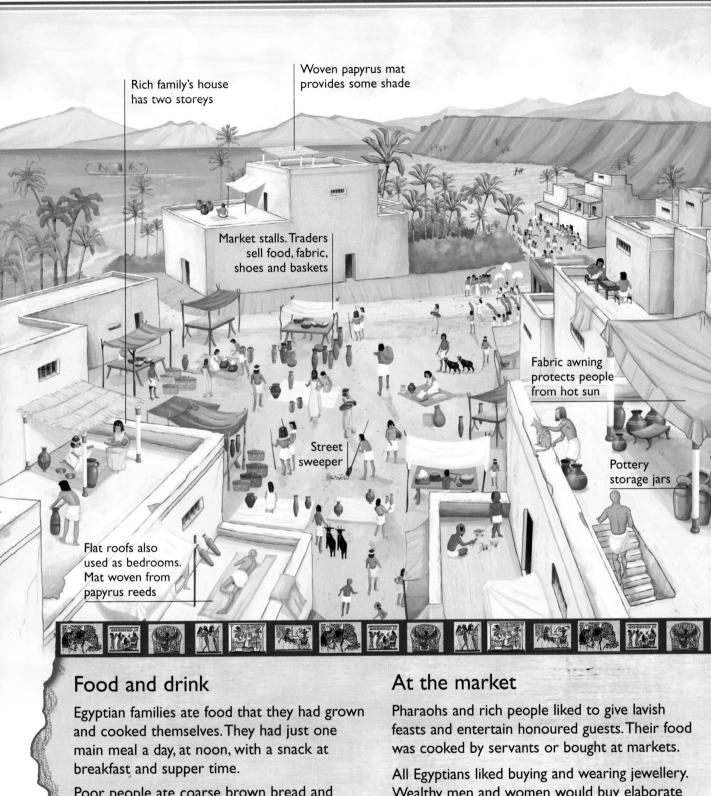

Rich family's house has two storeys

Woven papyrus mat provides some shade

Market stalls. Traders sell food, fabric, shoes and baskets

Fabric awning protects people from hot sun

Street sweeper

Pottery storage jars

Flat roofs also used as bedrooms. Mat woven from papyrus reeds

Food and drink

Egyptian families ate food that they had grown and cooked themselves. They had just one main meal a day, at noon, with a snack at breakfast and supper time.

Poor people ate coarse brown bread and vegetables – usually onions, garlic, lettuces, cucumbers and beans – washed down with thick, sweet beer. For a treat, they enjoyed fish and fruit, especially dates, grapes and melons.

At the market

Pharaohs and rich people liked to give lavish feasts and entertain honoured guests. Their food was cooked by servants or bought at markets.

All Egyptians liked buying and wearing jewellery. Wealthy men and women would buy elaborate collars, rings and bracelets or have them made. Poorer people wore simple pieces of jewellery bought from market stalls.

Make Egyptian jewellery

This project shows you how to make an Egyptian collar and some bracelets to complete your Ancient Egyptian outfit (see pages 8–9). The Egyptians loved gold, and used it in all sorts of jewellery, from earrings and belts to necklaces and hair ornaments.

Stylish designs

This pendant is from the tomb of the pharaoh Tutankhamun. It shows a vulture and is made of gold inlaid with blue and red semi-precious stones – lapis lazuli and cornelian. The gold to make jewellery came from mines between the River Nile and the Red Sea. Semi-precious stones were found in the deserts, or were imported.

The king ▶ would often give people a gift of jewellery, if they had served the state well.

Collar

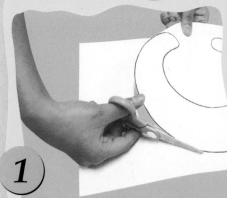

1

Draw a collar shape on some thick, white card, as shown above. The collar should be big enough to fit around your neck. Cut it out.

Bracelets

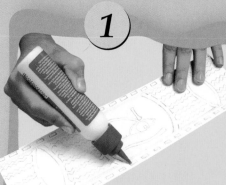

1

Cut out strips of card about 8cm deep and long enough to fit comfortably around your wrist, with an extra 2cm overlap. Draw designs on the card with PVA glue squeezed through a tube.

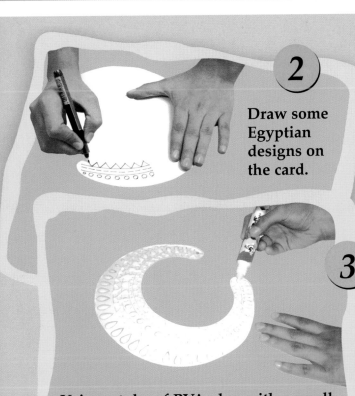

2

Draw some Egyptian designs on the card.

4

Ask an adult to make holes at each end, using a hole punch. Thread some cord through the holes so you can fasten the collar around your neck.

3

Using a tube of PVA glue with a small nozzle, squeeze out the glue to make a pattern of raised lines. Leave it to dry for several hours, then paint the whole collar with gold paint. When dry, paint the raised pattern with bright colours.

2

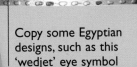

Copy some Egyptian designs, such as this 'wedjet' eye symbol

When dry, paint in gold. Add touches of paint in other colours, such as blue, red and turquoise. Glue the edges of the card together, to make a bracelet.

You will need

- Thick, white card
- Scissors
- PVA glue (in a tube with a nozzle)
- Metallic paints
- Fine-tipped paintbrush
- Hole punch
- Cord

Friends and family

Egyptians were lively, sociable people. They enjoyed family life, and sharing work or leisure-time with friends. They celebrated weddings and religious festivals with parties, singing and dancing.

▲ This family statue of Ka-em-heset shows him with his wife and son. Ka-em-heset was the chief sculptor and royal architect around 2300 BC. Families paid for carved and painted stone statues like this to be placed in their tombs, so that their spirits could all be together in the Afterlife.

Family life

Families were partnerships. Each member had a job to do, and a duty to help all the others. Men worked in the fields, in workshops or on building sites. Women cooked, cleaned, cared for babies, brewed beer, spun thread and wove fabric. Children learned from their parents, and worked for them.

Boys and girls could marry for love, though some marriages were arranged by parents. Divorce was allowed for cruelty. A typical couple might wed at 12 years of age – and be dead soon after 30! Many women died in childbirth; men in accidents or war. Disease killed many children; only the strongest survived.

▼ Adults and children loved sports, such as ball-games, leapfrog and tug-of-war. Children played with dolls and model animals, such as this wooden lion. Families also played board games, such as Senet and Snake.

▲ Dressed in their best, men and women guests sit chatting at a feast. Boy servants and young women offer them food and drink.

Party dress made of fine, lightweight, pleated linen

Guest sniffs a scented flower. The Egyptians loved perfumes

Servant girl hands a drinking-cup to a guest. Wine was for rich people or special occasions only

Family pets and other animals

Egyptians lived close to animals, on their farms and beside the Nile. Farm animals and pets were useful and beautiful, but wild creatures were dangerous and feared.

Children playing in the fields were often killed by scorpion stings and snakebites, or infected by disease-carrying flies. People washing in the river had their legs bitten off by hippos and crocodiles.

Cats (called 'miw') killed the rats and mice that ate farmers' grain. Egyptians were the first to tame cats; they also worshipped a cat-goddess called Bastet.

Dogs (called 'iwiw') were used for hunting, tracking criminals and guarding homes. Tombstones for pet dogs still survive, inscribed with names such as 'Brave One' and 'Trusty'.

Play 'Snake'

Board games were popular with lots of Egyptian families. One of the oldest so far discovered is called 'Snake' because the stone board it is played on looks like a coiled snake. This project shows you how to make a board and counters so you can play a game of Snake.

How to play Snake

No one knows for sure how the Ancient Egyptians played Snake. However, you can play a game for two players using these simple rules:

- **Each player has four balls, or counters, which should be placed on the snake's tail.**
- **Each player throws the dice to decide who starts. The person throwing the highest score begins.**
- **Take turns to throw the dice. Each player must throw a six before they can move a ball from the tail on to the snake's body.**
- **The balls must be moved one by one around the spiral towards the head, according to the number on the dice.**
- **Whoever throws a six gets another turn.**
- **If a player lands on a square occupied by another player, the other player's ball goes back to the tail and the player must throw a six to bring it back into play.**
- **The winner is the first person to get all their four balls on to the snake's head.**

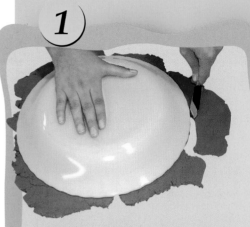

1

Roll out a large piece of modelling clay, 3cm thick and more than 30cm wide. Place a dinner plate or bowl upside-down on the clay and ask an adult to cut around it with a blunt knife.

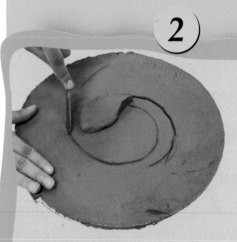

2

Model a snake's head and fix it on to the centre of the clay circle with some water. You could give the snake two glass bead eyes. Lightly trace out the snake's spiral body with the tip of a blunt knife.

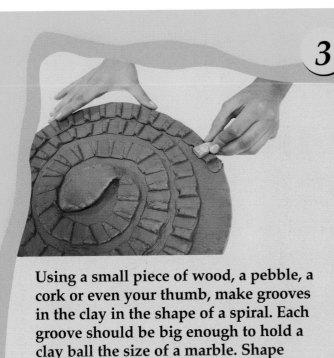

3

Using a small piece of wood, a pebble, a cork or even your thumb, make grooves in the clay in the shape of a spiral. Each groove should be big enough to hold a clay ball the size of a marble. Shape a piece of clay to make the tip of the snake's tail, then leave the clay board to harden.

You will need

- Self-hardening modelling clay (in three different colours)
- Rolling pin
- Large dinner plate or bowl
- Blunt knife or palette knife
- A small piece of wood, a pebble or a cork
- Two glass beads or pebbles (for the snake's eyes)
- Gold paint and brush
- Dice (to play the game!)

4

Roll eight marble-sized balls out of clay, four in one colour and four in another. Flatten the bases a little, so they don't roll off the board. Leave to dry, then paint Egyptian designs on them in gold metallic paint.

Writing, counting and discovering

The Ancient Egyptians were some of the first people to invent writing, yet few could read or write. Ordinary people memorized useful knowledge, family history, jokes, stories and songs, and passed them on by word of mouth.

▲ Hieroglyphs carved on smooth stone, at a temple. Egyptians believed that each sign had the power to do good or ill, like the person, object or thought it stood for.

Scribe

◀ Schools for scribes belonged to temples. They were known as 'Houses of Life'. Boys learned to read and write in groups by copying and reciting texts. They started to train as scribes when they were 12 years old.

Hieroglyph (picture symbol)

Students, all boys

Stone palette to hold black and red ink

Students practised writing on broken bits of stone called ostaca

Egyptian children's hairstyle. Boys have shaven heads, except for one lock of hair

Pen, made from reed stalk

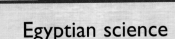

Egyptian science

Medicine
Egyptians did not understand how many body parts worked, or what caused diseases. They treated patients with herbal medicines, prayers, amulets (charms) and magic spells.

Maths and engineering
Massive monuments, such as the pyramids, show the Egyptians' skills at surveying and calculating. They used a decimal system of numbering, and discovered how to work out the area of squares, circles and triangles.

Astronomy and prediction
Priests observed the stars and planets very closely, and used them to invent a calendar. This helped them work out when the Nile was likely to flood. They also invented the Nilometer to measure the depth of the Nile floodwaters. About 6 or 7 metres of floodwater were needed to be sure of a good harvest.

Reading and writing

Only boys from rich families learned to read and write. They needed these skills for a high-ranking career. Trained scribes (writers) also copied out royal commands, religious texts, laws, letters, poems and books about magic, medicine and science.

Egyptians used three scripts. Hieroglyphics (picture-writing) was for carving royal or religious texts in stone; each symbol stood for an object or idea. Hieratic (simplified hieroglyphs, with flowing shapes) was for writing with pen and ink. Demotic (even simpler, and quick) was used for letters and business documents.

Scrolls of papyrus, covered with writing

Painted plaster statue of a scribe. Scribes usually ▲ sat cross-legged on the ground like this. Egyptians did not use desks or tables for writing.

Make a lucky pendant

The Ancient Egyptians sometimes wrote protective spells in hieroglyphs on papyrus, to keep them safe. The papyrus was then rolled up and carried in a pendant worn around the neck. Here's how to make your own lucky pendant.

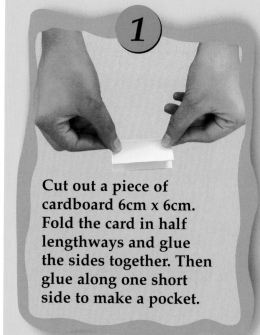

1

Cut out a piece of cardboard 6cm x 6cm. Fold the card in half lengthways and glue the sides together. Then glue along one short side to make a pocket.

Egyptian amulets

An amulet was a charm to ward off evil. The 'wedjet' eye charm represented the eye of the sun-god Amun-Re and the god Horus. The scarab beetle represented the sun-god Khepri. Only kings and queens were allowed to carry the ankh, the Egyptian symbol of life.

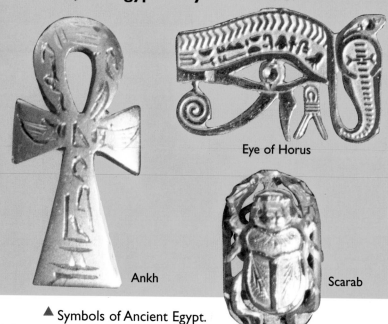

Ankh

Eye of Horus

Scarab

▲ Symbols of Ancient Egypt.

3

Cut out a small rectangle of card measuring 4cm x 1cm for the hanging loop. Cover it in gold foil, then fold it in half and glue it to the back of the pendant, at the top (see picture below). Cover the rest of the pendant in gold foil and smooth it down.

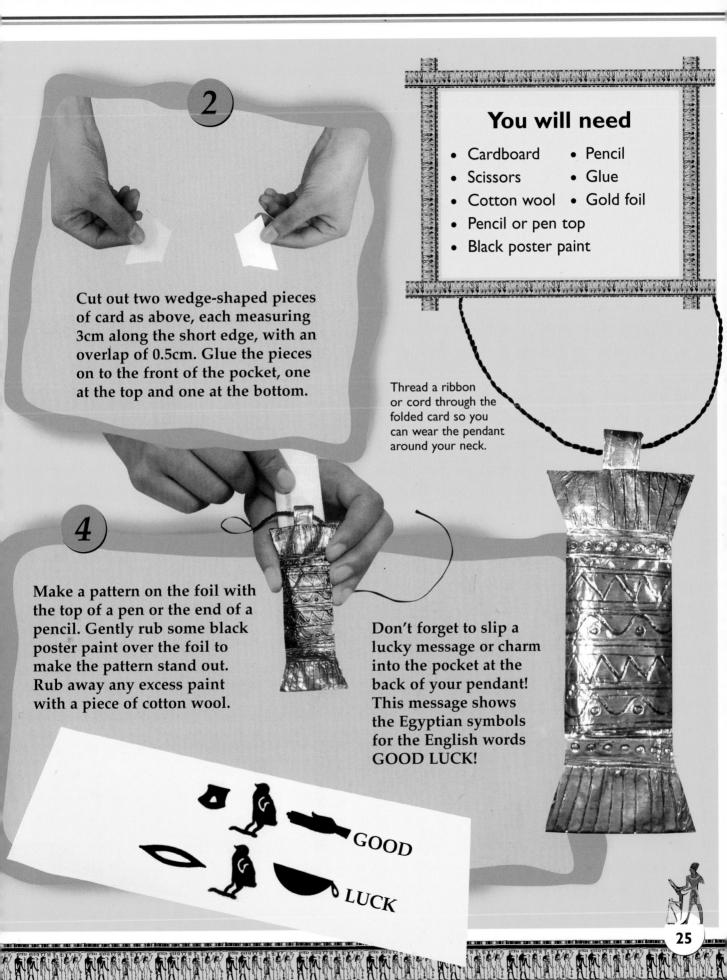

2

Cut out two wedge-shaped pieces of card as above, each measuring 3cm along the short edge, with an overlap of 0.5cm. Glue the pieces on to the front of the pocket, one at the top and one at the bottom.

You will need

- Cardboard
- Scissors
- Cotton wool
- Pencil or pen top
- Black poster paint
- Pencil
- Glue
- Gold foil

Thread a ribbon or cord through the folded card so you can wear the pendant around your neck.

4

Make a pattern on the foil with the top of a pen or the end of a pencil. Gently rub some black poster paint over the foil to make the pattern stand out. Rub away any excess paint with a piece of cotton wool.

Don't forget to slip a lucky message or charm into the pocket at the back of your pendant! This message shows the Egyptian symbols for the English words GOOD LUCK!

GOOD

LUCK

25

Everlasting life

The Egyptians feared death, and hoped to live for ever. They believed this would happen if their bodies were preserved as a shelter for their 'ka' (spirit) in the Afterlife.

Death and burial

At first, bodies were preserved by burying them in the desert. The dry sand stopped them rotting away. Later, pharaohs and rich people paid to have their bodies made into mummies, then safely buried in strong or secret tombs.

Mummy-makers removed a body's inner organs, dried its flesh with natron, injected it with plant oils and wrapped it in layers of bandages, often with amulets placed between the layers. Finally, the mummy was sealed in a coffin decorated with the dead person's portrait and pictures of guardian gods.

The mummy of ▲ Pharaoh Rameses II (ruled 1279–1213 BC), which has survived for over 3,000 years. It was unwrapped a long time ago.

◄ Family members taking part in an 'Opening of the Mouth' ceremony for a dead relative. They gently touch the mummy with special holy knives. They believe this will let the mummy's 'ka' (spirit) enter its body, and let the dead person live again.

Priestess kneeling and saying prayers. Rich people paid for crowds of mourners to weep and pray at their funerals

Mummy is coated in black resin (plant gum or oil) to preserve it. For the Egyptians, black was a symbol of rebirth, like the rich, dark Nile mud

▲ Priests carry newly made mummies, wrapped in cloth and bandages. Next, each mummy will be carried to its tomb, accompanied by mourners and musicians chanting prayers, and laid to rest in a wooden coffin or stone sarcophagus.

Gods and goddesses

Magical, mysterious, beyond their control – that's how Egyptians saw the world. So they asked gods and goddesses for help:

Amun (king or ram) creator god

Anubis (jackal) god of dead bodies

Bastet (cat) household goddess

Bes (dwarf) god of children

Hathor (cow) goddess of music and love

Horus (hawk) god of the sky

Isis (mother) goddess of healing

Maat (woman or feather) goddess of truth and justice

Osiris (king) god of the Afterlife

Ra (man with hawk's or ram's head) god of the sun

Thoth (bird) god of scribes

Make a mummy mask

Before a mummified body was sealed in a coffin and laid in a tomb, its face was often covered with a beautiful, lifelike mask. This was to make sure the dead person would be recognised in the Afterlife. The simplest masks were made of plaster. Others were painted wood. The finest were made of gleaming gold, decorated with semi-precious stones. This project shows you how to make a papier-mâché mummy mask.

Tutankhamun's mask

Tutankhamun became pharaoh when he was just nine years old. When he died at the age of 18, his body was made into a mummy then put into three coffins that fitted one inside the other. This famous gold death mask was found in his tomb.

 ▲ This life-size mask protected Tutankhamun's mummy. It was made of gold and inlaid with semi-precious stones.

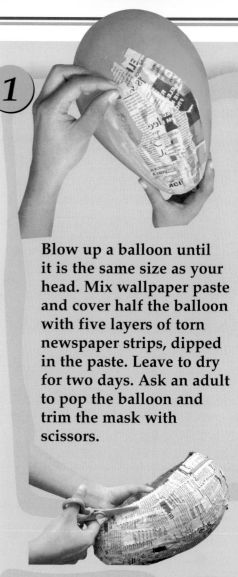

1

Blow up a balloon until it is the same size as your head. Mix wallpaper paste and cover half the balloon with five layers of torn newspaper strips, dipped in the paste. Leave to dry for two days. Ask an adult to pop the balloon and trim the mask with scissors.

3

When dry, cut out the headdress shape (this is like a horseshoe) from thick card and glue it in place behind the mask. When dry, cover the mask and headdress in two or three layers of white emulsion.

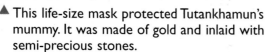

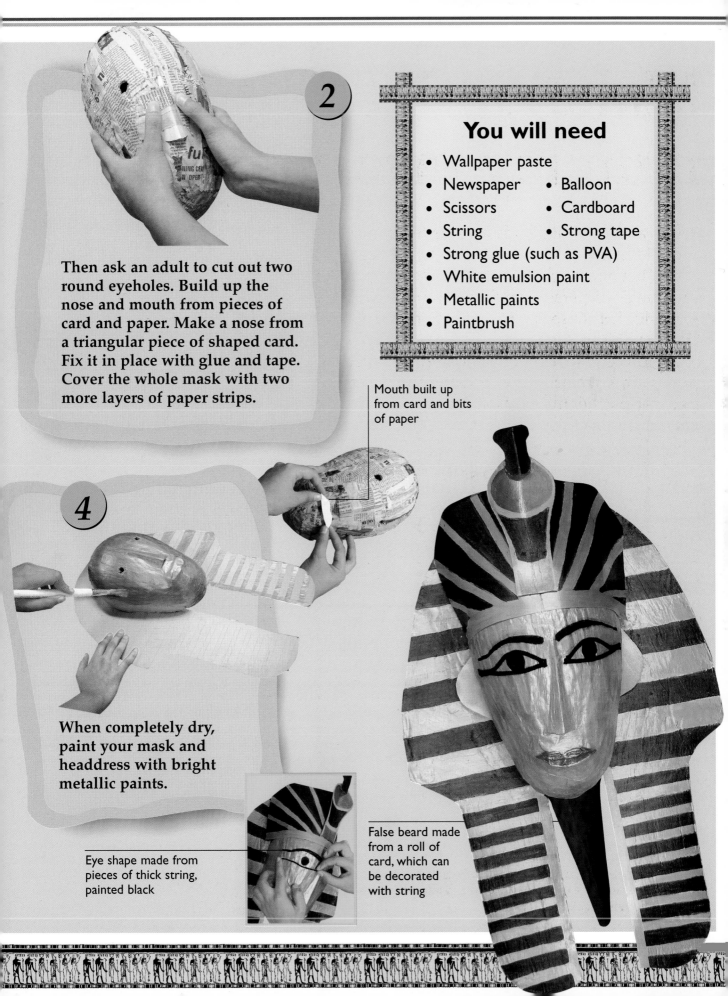

2

Then ask an adult to cut out two round eyeholes. Build up the nose and mouth from pieces of card and paper. Make a nose from a triangular piece of shaped card. Fix it in place with glue and tape. Cover the whole mask with two more layers of paper strips.

Mouth built up from card and bits of paper

You will need

- Wallpaper paste
- Newspaper
- Balloon
- Scissors
- Cardboard
- String
- Strong tape
- Strong glue (such as PVA)
- White emulsion paint
- Metallic paints
- Paintbrush

4

When completely dry, paint your mask and headdress with bright metallic paints.

Eye shape made from pieces of thick string, painted black

False beard made from a roll of card, which can be decorated with string

Timeline

c. **10000–8000** BC Climate change turns 90 per cent of Egypt into desert.

c. **5500** BC Egyptian farmers plant crops, raise animals, build villages beside Nile.

c. **3500** BC The first Egyptian walled towns.

c. **3100** BC Upper (southern) and Lower (northern) Egypt unite. The new kingdom is ruled by pharaohs from capital city, Memphis.

2686–2181 BC Old Kingdom. Pyramids built as tombs for pharaohs.

2181–2055 BC Wars in Egypt between rival leaders.

2055–1650 BC Middle Kingdom. Pharaohs conquer Nubia, and pay for splendid temples and statues. Capital city moved to Thebes. Egypt trades with Middle East.

1650–1550 BC Hyksos (people from Palestine) settle in Egypt and grow powerful.

1550–1069 BC New Kingdom. Pharaohs conquer and rule a great empire, and defeat invaders. Tutankhamun's tomb and other royal burials in the Valley of the Kings. Egypt trades with Africa and Mediterranean lands.

1069–747 BC Pharaohs rule northern Egypt; kings from Nubia rule southern Egypt.

747–332 BC Egypt is rich, but losing power. It is invaded by Assyrians (from Syria and Iraq) and Persians (from Iran).

332–30 BC Egypt is conquered by King Alexander the Great of Macedonia (north of Greece), and ruled by Macedonians, including Queen Cleopatra VII.

30 BC–AD **395** Egypt is conquered by Rome, and becomes part of the Roman Empire.

AD **324** Christianity becomes the official religion of Egypt.

AD **641** Arab invaders bring Islam and the Arabic language to Egypt.

Glossary

Amulet Lucky charm. Small object or image believed to have protective powers.

Fertile (soil) Containing all that is needed to grow strong, healthy plants.

Inner organs All parts of the body that are not skin, muscle, bone or hair. Egyptians removed the brain, lungs, liver, stomach and intestines when making mummies, but left the heart in place. They thought it contained the dead person's mind.

Inscription Writing carved on stone.

Irrigation Bringing water to dry land, to help crops grow.

Ka Spirit. The Egyptians believed that a person was made of five things: body, ka (spirit), ba (personality), name, shadow.

Natron Salty chemical, found in Egyptian deserts. Mummy-makers used it to absorb moisture from dead bodies.

Nubia Land to the south of Ancient Egypt; today, it is part of Egypt and Sudan.

Papyrus A type of reed (tall, grass-like plant) that grew beside the River Nile. The Ancient Egyptians flattened and pressed its stalks to make paper.

Pharaoh The Ancient Egyptians' name for their king.

Reservoir Artificial, man-made lake, used to store water.

Scribes Professional writers. In Egypt, most scribes worked as government officials.

Shrine Holy place, usually inside a temple, where the statue of a god or goddess was kept.

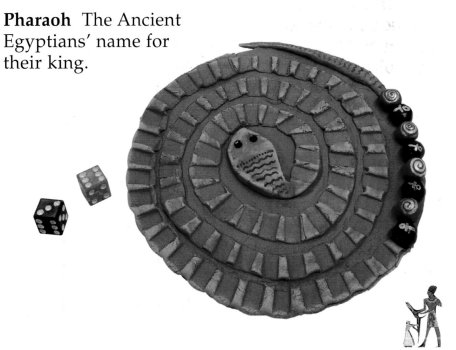

Index

Abu Simbel 5
Abydos 5
Akenhaten 7
Akhet 11
Alexander the Great 30
Amenhotep I 7
amulet 24, 26, 31
Amun 27
ankh 24
Anubis 27
Assyrians 30

Bastet 19, 27
Bes 27

Cleopatra VII 7, 30
cornelian 16

demotic script 23

eagle collar 8

Giza 4, 5
Great Pyramid 4, 5, 7

Hathor 27
Hatshepsut 5, 7
hieratic script 23
hieroglyphs 6, 22, 23
Horus 6, 24, 27
Hyksos 30

Isis 5, 27
iwiw 19

ka 18, 26, 27, 31
Ka-em-heset 18
Khepri 24
Khufu 7

Maat 27

Macedonia 30
Memphis 5, 30
miw 19
mummy 3, 4, 26, 27, 28, 31
mummy-makers 26, 31

Narmer 7
New Kingdom 30
Nile River 4, 5, 10, 16, 31
Nubia 5, 7, 30, 31

Old Kingdom 30
Opening of the Mouth 27
Osiris 27

papyrus 10, 12, 15, 23, 24, 31

Peret 11
Philae 5

Ra 27
Rameses II 5, 26
Red Sea 5, 16

Saqqara 5

Temple of Isis 5
Thebes 5, 30
Thoth 27
Thutmose III 7
Tutankhamun 5, 16, 28, 30

Valley of the Kings 7, 30

wedjet 17, 24

Webfinder

http://www.ancientegypt.co.uk
The British Museum gives information on Egyptian life, gods and goddesses, mummification, pharaohs, pyramids, temples and lots more.

http://www.bbc.co.uk/history/ancient/egyptians/
Pyramid challenge, Be a mummy maker, Explore the treasures of Tutankhamun, Health hazards cures in Ancient Egypt, Hieroglyphics – write your name in the ancient script.

http://www.historyforkids.org/learn/egypt/
Crafts, projects and lots of information about Ancient Egypt.

http://www.iwebquest.com/egypt/ancientegypt.htm
Information about daily life in Ancient Egypt, plus activities and missions.